# Words of Wisdom
*What you need to know on the road of your life's journey*

By: Amy L. Fuentes

© 2019 by Amy L. Fuentes.

All rights reserved. No part of this publication may be reproduced, stored in a retrieval system, transmitted, or otherwise be copied for public or private use, in any form or by any means, electronic, mechanical, photocopying, recording, or otherwise--except for brief quotation in printed reviews, without the prior written permission of the author, Amy Fuentes.

You are on a journey called life. This adventure will be amazing and to help you along the way there are a few items you should always remember. They say a picture is worth a thousand words, so pictures accompany the "Words of Wisdom" shared in this book.

It is my hope that the contents of this book remind you of what you may already know and enlighten you to some things you may not have considered at the time when you need to hear them.

**You are truly amazing just the way you are.**

Daily you will come into contact with people who will tell you otherwise – teachers, friends, bosses, boyfriends, etc. Close your eyes and look inside and you will see what your friends and family already see, an incredibly capable, caring, smart, loving, wonderful person!

## Only **YOU** can make you happy.

Being skinnier, prettier, richer, or having the greatest job or the best boyfriend is not going to make you happy. Sure, they certainly will enhance your life, but happiness comes from within and the sooner you discover what exactly makes you happy the sooner you can make sure you incorporate this into your life on a daily basis.

**Don't let others bring you down, instead bring them up.**

It seems much more hip to sit around and complain about life. While it is normal to want and strive for more, always remember how rich your life is right now. To help you when you are down about your life, sit and think of at least 10 things for which you are grateful or happy and review and build on it every day. Start out slow like the fact that you woke up today, had something to eat, had clothes to wear, have people in your life who care about you, and go from there. A great time to do this is before you go to bed or when you wake up.

 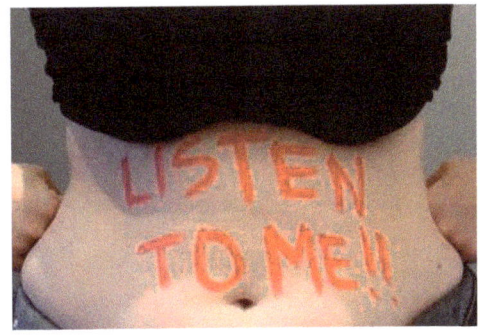

## Listen to your head, but trust your gut!

If something doesn't feel quite right, don't do it.
Your gut is typically correct, so don't ignore it.

**When you are sad, sing!**

It seems simple, but singing, especially a favorite childhood song that you love, seems to start you on the right path for bringing a smile to your face and laughter to your day.

**Bring a smile to someone's day
and it will be returned to you ten-fold.**

Tell someone a joke, help people bring their groceries inside or just open a door for someone. Helping others gives you a euphoric feeling that will make you feel good for hours after.

## Plan, Prepare, but don't be scared to JUMP!

You can think about and analyze a situation, you can plan and prepare for something, but don't have analysis paralysis…be sure once you have thought it all through that you jump in 100% and give it your all!

**Live with no regrets.**

Make the best decision you can at the time you need to make it with the information you have and then don't look back, just keep looking forward.

**What can be done can also be undone.**

If you make a decision that ends up not to be the best, change it. If you buy a home you decide you don't like, sell it. If you buy a car that ends up costing too much money, sell it and get a different one. If you take a job you don't like or work for a person you don't care for and can't make it work or move within the company, get a new job.

**Live in the moment.**

Please don't take on so many responsibilities and fill your day and your life with numerous obligations that you're constantly thinking of what you need to do instead of doing what you need. By always thinking of what else needs to be done, you can't possibly enjoy what you are doing at the moment.

**Enjoy every day.**

Try to incorporate at least one person or event into your day that makes you laugh or at least smile. At the end of the day it is better to have these wonderful moments to remember and they help you look forward to the following day.

**Spending time with those you love
is what's most important.**

In the end, this will mean more than money or fame,
expensive cars or homes, jewelry or trips to exotic places.

## Your thought and time are the two best gifts.

Sure a trip around the world, a fancy car, and beautiful jewelry are nice, but the best gift you can give is time from your busy schedule to think about someone and spend time with him/her. It doesn't have to be extravagant or expensive.  It can be as simple as making lemonade and spending an hour on a porch with someone you care about.

## Communication is the key.

All relationships including friends, spouse, siblings, parents, boss, workers, and clients require constant and clear communication. So talk often and let others know what you're thinking, expecting, and wanting.

**It's not what you say but how you say it.**

In order for your message to be heard it is best to say it in a way that the person can hear it.  So, think a moment about the best way to say it.  If it is not heard correctly, (you can tell by the person's body language or reaction) take the time to clarify what you were trying to say.

### God gave us two ears and one mouth...

so you should listen twice as much as you speak. It's amazing what you hear when you stop talking and take the time to really listen.

**Honesty is the best policy.**

But remember, it's not what you say but how you say it,
so you don't hurt someone's feelings.

**This too shall pass.**

When life gets tough, which it definitely will, remember to keep things in perspective and know that whatever it is that is happening, it will eventually pass. Funny how life hands you difficulties in order to build your character, give you confidence, and allow you to have experiences that will come in handy at another time in your life. And rest assured that it always works out.

# Don't quit

When things go wrong, as they sometimes will,
When the road you're trudging seems all uphill,
When the funds are low and the debts are high,
And you want to smile, but you have to sigh,
When care is pressing you down a bit
Rest if you must, but don't you quit.

Life is queer with its twists and its turns,
As everyone of us sometimes learns,
And many a failure turns about
When they might have won, had they stuck it out.
Don't give up though the pace seems slow,
You may succeed with another blow.

Often the goal is nearer than,
It seems to a faint and faltering man,
Often the struggler has given up
When he might have captured the victor's cup;
And he learned too late when the night came down,
How close he was to the golden crown.

Success is failure turned inside out
The silver tint of the clouds of doubt
And you never can tell how close you are,
It may be near when it seems so far;
So stick to the fight when you're hardest hit,
It's when things seem worst that you must not quit!

## Don't quit!

Life is going to get tough and when it does buckle down and do what you need to in order to complete what you started.  However, there are definitely times when you need to stop doing something whether a project, job, friendship, or relationship, due to lack of funds or time, conflicts, health or changing priorities.  Be sure to give it your all, but also know when it is time to walk away.

**When faced with a problem or situation you have two options, accept it or change it but don't complain and wallow in it.**

It is truly a waste of your time.

**Believe in yourself.**

When self-confidence is waning just remember, there are people who have done whatever it is you are trying to do who are less intelligent, less prepared, less capable, have less money, have less support and resources, and they do just fine.  So if they can do it, you can too!

**You can do anything you put your mind to…
absolutely anything!**

And don't you let anyone, including yourself,
tell you anything different.

# it ALWAYS SEEMS IMPOSSIBLE UNTIL it is DONE.

**Anything worth doing is worth doing 100%.**

Decide whether or not you're going to do something and then give it your all. If you're just going to do it half way, don't do it at all!

**I DON'T MAKE EXCUSES I MAKE RESULTS**

**Look for the silver lining in bad situations.**

Although it is not always easy, realize that things happen for a reason; you have to learn something, or experience something for some event later in life that may not be obvious to you now. So when life gives you lemons, make lemonade. Look at the situation and see what good has come out of it or what you have learned that you can utilize at another time or use to help someone else. This will help you get through the tough times.

## Fake it 'til you make it.

Whenever you do something for the first time,
especially a job, you may want to pretend you're
confident and self-assured even though you
may not feel that way. After all, you don't have
to be confident; you just have to project confidence.
Your confidence will come as you gain experience;
so until you get it, fake it.

## When in doubt, do nothing.

If you are unsure which road to take, have a seat
and wait until you feel comfortable. This is true
with relationships, confrontations, decisions on
jobs, what car to buy, etc. If you close your eyes
and sit quietly many times the answer
you are looking for will appear.

**You get more with honey than with vinegar.**

Many times people make us mad and we just want
to yell at them and give them a piece of our mind.
Try to resist the urge to do this and instead
take a deep breath and speak nicely. Speaking civilly
will get you more than if you scream and yell.
And you never know when you may
need their help in the future.

**Never burn any bridges.**

This applies more to jobs and friendships.
Sometimes these come to an end and when they do
be sure to end it on a good note. You never know
when you may run into that person or need that person's
help and it will be easier if you left on good terms.

**You're like those you hang around.**

This is also called guilt by association.
So be sure to hang around fun, happy, successful,
well-connected, generous, good-natured,
thoughtful people like you!

**People come into our lives for
a reason, a season or a lifetime.**

Not all friendships are golden and last forever.
So enjoy the people when they are in your life
and let them go when it is time.

## A leopard never changes his spots.

If a person is a liar or a cheater he/she will always be a liar or a cheater. Very few people are able to make serious changes in behavior or personality. Always be leery and keep your guard up if you run into someone that you knew in the past was not a good person, lied, cheated, etc.

## You can't change a person, but you can change how you think and interact with that person.

We have no control over others but we certainly have control
over our thoughts of them and how we decide to interpret situations.
All of us have quirks and some of them may bother others. Remember
this when you are in the company of people who have aspects of their
personality that grate on your nerves. Instead of choosing to be irritated
by their comments and actions or taking them personally,
try to take them in stride and appreciate the parts of their
personality you enjoy. The choice of how you react
to people and events in your life is yours.

## Treat your family and your eventual spouse like you do your friends.

Don't take them for granted and be sure to treat them with respect. Thank them when they do something nice for you. Give them the benefit of the doubt and the opportunity to explain when something seems wrong. Forgive them when they make a mistake or are in a foul mood. Speak to them in a manner and tone that you would a friend. Many times we treat horribly those we love the most. We take out our bad day on them or we get short and snippy with them when we are tired or hungry. Try really hard not to do this. Before you open your mouth, ask yourself if you would say what you're about to say to a friend. And since we are all human, when you do treat those you love poorly, apologize.

**Find the positive in every person and situation.**

Sure everyone has positives and negatives, and we can't change that. So focus on the positives and downplay or disregard the negatives as long as they are not serious, life threatening or dangerous. Hopefully, the positives outweigh the negatives.

**You can choose your friends,
but you can't choose your family.**

Through thick and through thin, your family will be there for you.
Sometimes they may piss you off and/or disappoint you.
When they do, be sure to nicely tell them,
but then forgive them and move on.

**No one is perfect, not even you!**

Most of us do our best, but we are all human and we all make mistakes. Forgive others, but most importantly, forgive yourself!

**Rome was not built in a day!**

God did not create everything in one day either.
Your goals may take awhile to achieve, but don't give up.
Keep working toward them and you will achieve them!

**You are loved!**

In case no one has told you today, you are an outstanding and upstanding person and loved for all you bring to this world. The world is a better place because you are in it!

www.ingramcontent.com/pod-product-compliance
Ingram Content Group UK Ltd.
Pitfield, Milton Keynes, MK11 3LW, UK
UKHW062044180426
11947UKWH00030B/2042